CW00376844

Union

God

Living the Christ Life

by Fr David Vincent Meconi SJ

To the Olsens, my *icon oxoniensis*
of the holy Family

*All booklets are published thanks to the
generous support of the members of the
Catholic Truth Society*

CATHOLIC TRUTH SOCIETY
PUBLISHERS TO THE HOLY SEE

Contents

The Divine Plan of Salvation 3

The Great Exchange..19

New Creatures in the Spirit of Holiness....................33

Seeking the Grace of Union 43

Fr David Vincent Meconi SJ is a member of the Chicago Province (USA) of the Society of Jesus, currently residing at Campion Hall, Oxford. Apart from his many pastoral duties, his academic specialty is the thought of St Augustine of Hippo as well as the place of prayer and the emergence of a Christian culture in the early Church.

The Divine Plan of Salvation

Do you have a personal relationship with Jesus Christ?

This question, posed to me while out on a walk through the winding paths of Scotland's St Andrew's University, became a true moment of grace. My reply to this friendly evangelist was that in fact I did have a relationship but, adding remorsefully, 'it is *not* a relationship with Jesus I want.' To her ever-growing alarm, I went on to tell her that, 'With Mother Mary and with you and with all the saints I want a relationship, but with Jesus I want union. I desire something even more intimate than relationship. I do not want to be simply face to face with Jesus, or side to side: I want his face to become my face: his heart to beat in perfect harmony with mine. With St Paul, I want to be able to say that it is no longer I who live but Christ who lives in me (cf. *Gal* 2:20). I want divine union.' She abruptly thanked me for our conversation and, obviously still a bit flummoxed, proceeded to hand me some tracts regarding providence and God's plan for my life.

Years later, I still chuckle when I picture her face as I tried to explain what I meant and, more importantly, I continue to pray in gratitude for her, for she was a Christian woman who was in love with her faith but someone who did not understand the Faith deeply. While examining my conscience later that night, I was blessed with an intimate awareness of how the desire I voiced was precisely what the ancient Church meant by our 'becoming God', by deification, divinisation, or *theosis*, as it is known in the East. At that moment a medieval Latin phrase came back to me, formulating very aptly what I was trying to say - *Christianus, alter Christus* - a Christian is another Christ!

Not familiar with this type of language, my evangelist's suspicion was to be expected. But such strict identity between God and his friends is on every page of solid Christian theology. "Let us rejoice then and give thanks that we have become not only Christians, but Christ himself" (St Augustine, d. 431, *Commentary on John* 21.8; quoted at *CCC* 795), or as St Cyril of Jerusalem (d. 387) put it, "So then you who have become sharers in Christ are appropriately called Christs" (*Mystagogical Catecheses* 3.1; quoted at *CCC* 2782). The hidden beauty of Jesus Christ is not only that he longs to live for you, it is not even that he lives with you or through you, but that he actually desires to

4

live *in* you and, we might dare to say, *as you*! He wants to make your life - in all of its various dimensions and in all of its joys and struggles - his own. Can we begin to fathom what that means? How do we become one with God and what do we mean when we say Christ wants to be wholly identified with his followers? Perhaps even more startling, what do we mean when we say that a Christian's primary vocation is to 'become God'?

This little book sets out to explore the Catholic Church's teaching on divine union. Living the Christ life is the consummation of the Christian promise: that we are to become one with God. While this may sound outlandish at first, it is not an altogether foreign idea. Reflect on your own experience. It occurs whenever two people in love spend time together - they become like one another. Or as the founder of *Communion and Liberation*, Luigi Giussani (d. 2005), expressed in a letter to a close companion, "The aspiration of friendship is union, it is that of becoming identified, becoming part of each other, becoming the same person, assuming the same physiognomy of the friend" (*Letter of Faith and Friendship* as in *Traces* 7.3 [2005] 31). Certainly you are 'like' your best friend in many important ways, and if you are married, you have probably noticed that over the years, you and your spouse have become more and more similar in expectation and expression. Well, in Jesus

Christ, God has become like us and in our lives of Christian charity and sacramental worship, we are invited to become like God. In Christ we are called to become perfect as our heavenly Father is perfect (cf. *Mt* 5:48), to love as Jesus loves (cf. *Jn* 13:34), to be committed to the Faith and to glow ardently aflame with the Holy Spirit (cf. *Rom* 12:11). As is the case between you and your best friend, however, becoming like one another does not destroy your individuality but actually perfects it. This is the paradox of humanity's divinisation. Because we are created in God's own image and likeness, 'becoming God' does not abolish who we are but makes us who we have always been made to be.

Why deification?

Our becoming divine is the sole purpose for God's choosing to act outside of himself. It is the goal of his choosing to create the universe and why he became human in Christ Jesus: to give us a share in his divine nature. Deification is an arresting term capturing everything God has destined for us, everything Christ desires to achieve within us. What is the greatest gift God could ever bestow upon us? His ultimate gift to us is divine and living: it is God himself. God is not only the author of our salvation, he is our salvation. What more could we ever really desire? As splendid as the gifts of this world and our natural lives are, they are infinitely outmatched by the divine life God desires to pour into our souls.

This is what this *Deeper Christianity series* is all about: being drawn into the life of the Lord ever deeper by allowing him to be drawn into our life more intimately. If today the Christian is in need of clearer catechesis and direction, it is because most of contemporary Christianity has forgotten the glorious end for which God has acted. Our lives have been instilled with and directed toward a particular purpose. If we fulfil that goal, we enjoy eternal beatitude. If we fail, we do so at our own peril. Since we are created for divine union, this "intimate and vital bond" cannot "be forgotten, overlooked, or even explicitly rejected" (*CCC* 29). Of course we can choose to generate sufficient diversions so as never to have to lift our heads above our surrounding material, short-lived pleasures, but we can never really escape the true goal for which we have been created.

It is therefore of the utmost importance that Christians today be able to articulate why God has brought every human person into being. In his usual piercing manner, Blaise Pascal (1623-62) separates all of humanity by how each of us seeks the divine:

> "There are only three sorts of people: those who have found God and serve him; those who are busy seeking him and have not found him; those

who live without either seeking or finding him. The first are reasonable and happy, the last are foolish and unhappy, those in the middle are unhappy and reasonable" (*Pensées* §160).

Where are you? Can you honestly say that intimacy with God is your life's ultimate aim which guides all of your activities and provides you with an absolute target from which all your other (penultimate) goals are measured?

Resting the restless heart

The human person has an inescapable desire for perfect happiness. This yearning is common to all, regardless of race, creed or culture, because it is a "desire of divine origin" (*CCC* 1718) directing every human soul to the one true God. This is an essential insight, because before we start out on any endeavour or project, we must first understand the end we wish to achieve. 'Should I fly, take the bus, or ride my bike?' 'Well, that depends', the answer would come, 'Where is it you wish to go?'. Without a fixed goal clearly in mind, it is impossible to weigh intelligently or coherently between choices. Nothing can be understood fully until one understands the purpose for which it exists. Without a destination, a right turn is equally as good as a left, and eventually we find ourselves treating life as nothing more than an aimless joyride, having produced a generation chanting 'WHATEVER' as the slogan capturing their forlornness and spiritual torpor.

The great Christian masters have seen otherwise. For example, toward the beginning of his *Spiritual Exercises*, St Ignatius of Loyola (d. 1556) combats our fallen tendency to lose our way with this guideline:

> "The human person is created to praise, reverence and serve God Our Lord, and by so doing to save his or her soul. The other things on the face of the earth are created for human beings in order to help them pursue the end for which they are created. It follows from this that one must use other created things in so far as they help toward one's end, and free oneself from them in so far as they are obstacles to one's end" (*Principle and Foundation*; *Spiritual Exercises* §23).

Notice how Ignatius starts. Before entertaining *how* we should live, he first must establish why we are alive, "to praise, reverence and serve God". Our entire life must be directed toward that end, the only real and lasting goal we have. Once we are resolute on becoming saints, only then does it make sense to begin to make plans regarding all the "other things on the face of the earth". Always a master of human psychology, Ignatius opens with a clear proclamation that the goal of our lives is to praise and thus become the divine glory. This alone provides us with the aim toward which we should orient the whole of our lives' actions and desires.

Typical here too is the 'world friendliness' of St Ignatius. He never divides the world into anything automatically good or bad, nor does he ever list what created goods or activities will necessarily bring us closer to God. For Ignatius, any creature can prove to be either a holy icon inviting greater union with God or a deterrent to the divine, leading us away from the goal for which we should all be striving. Every seemingly mundane task can hence become, in the eyes of the saint, an opportunity to be used to grow in divine intimacy. Indeed, the saint is the one able to hear the sounds of the world as the primal symphony singing the glory of God.

Before entering the Jesuits I worked in the world of high finance on the floor of the Mercantile Exchange in Chicago. I came to see how one could become a saint amidst the chaos and the pressures but I just as quickly saw that I would not be one of them. I left the 'Merc' not because it was inherently bad but because it occasioned all the sins with which I (secretly but all too gladly) struggled - pride, control, greed, and selfishness. Upon joining religious life, many imagined I quit my job because I was too holy when, in fact, I left because I knew myself too weak. This experience gave me an insight into what Ignatius is saying here: first know that you are alive right now because God has made you to love him, and then know yourself well enough to understand what things assist in your loving God above all things and what things hinder you. If trading stocks brings you closer to God, be the best financier you can be; if not, turn away and embrace another means. The same, of course, goes for deciding whether one should enter religious life or not, get married or not, whether one should embrace wealth or poverty, health or sickness, and all the means God uses to call you into deeper communion with himself. Union begins with trust in God, knowledge of self and the discernment that bridges God's will with ours.

As we think about all of the different ways we are pulled in the course of an average day, of all the various attractions and aversions within us, we can better understand why we need one sovereign goal beyond which there is nothing left to strive. We all hunger for permanence and when we are honest, we see how the world cannot offer us the incorruptibility for which we all seek. "Now thus says the LORD of hosts: Consider your ways! You have sown much, but have brought in little; you have eaten, but have not been satisfied; you have drunk, but have not been exhilarated; have clothed yourselves, but not been warmed; And he who earned wages earned them for a bag with holes in it" (*Haggai* 1:5-6). Unless they are initiated, sustained and completed by the Lord, all earthly pursuits and relations leave us cold and empty, and as long as there is something still wanting, we are not yet at the Christ life. Union with the divine is the only state that can fulfil our deepest desires and give us a sense of purpose and peace. "Our hearts are restless until they rest in you", St Augustine confesses to God (*Confessions* 1.1), knowing how deep within the centre of the human heart is found a chamber opening up onto Infinity. It is God-sized and only God can fill it and until then, our vastness continues to hunger and ache - deep calling out to Deep (cf. *Ps* 42:7).

Sin: divine dissimilarity

Such yearning raises another advantage to thinking of the Christian life in terms of deification. It is an all too subtle trap to gauge one's spiritual journey solely in terms of the sins avoided. Combating personal sin is no doubt an essential part of following Christ, but it is nonetheless only the prelude to the fullness of life he offers us. So, let us then pray to be open to the graces which will burn out sin at every turn and out of every fibre of our being, for "no evil is graver than sin and nothing has worse consequences for sinners themselves, for the Church, and for the whole world" (*CCC* 1488). However, to envision the Christ life simply as shunning evil is like a builder who thinks he is finished with the house because the cellar has been made ready, forgetting that he has been employed for a much grander structure. Instead of gauging our lives in Christ simply by the sins we have avoided in the past 24 hours or so, we can now begin to think of the ways we are growing in order to be fully Christ-like. The essence of our Faith is neither the forgiveness of sins, nor is it even a peaceful reconciliation with God: what it means to be Christ's is to become other Christs!

So, while our desire for wholeness necessarily involves freedom from our sins, such absolution is only the beginning of the Christ life. The rest of that life consists in becoming like the One in whom alone our hearts can be satisfied. What is it we all want? We all want to know that someone rejoices in our very being, delights in us, and that in this someone we can wholly collapse and be accepted without reserve. The human heart wants its weaknesses and vulnerabilities to be understood without condition and its sins to be known without horror. In those rare moments when we are truly honest with ourselves, we all see that our most lasting desire is to love and to be loved. We yearn to belong to such mutuality, to know that we have been desired unrestrictedly - personally, perfectly, uniquely and forever. This is the essence of deification: it is the grace to enter into an eternal love affair and, in so doing, experience completion by sharing in absolute life. "I have come so that you may have life and have it to the full" (cf. *Jn* 10:10).

Anything less than this divine intimacy would leave us longing for more, unsatisfied and incomplete.

The triune life of love

We experience this longing for intimacy because our very being is patterned on the most loving act of self-gift imaginable. Because the Trinity freely wills "to communicate the glory of his blessed life" (*CCC* 257), God created other selves so as to lift them up "into the perfect unity of the Blessed Trinity" (*CCC* 260). This connection the *Catechism* makes between the intra-Trinitarian life and God's good creation proves essential for our study. The Trinity is constituted by a mutual sharing of persons: the Father is the Father precisely because he is received and thus confirmed by the Son, the Son is Son wholly due to this self-abandonment of the Father, and the Holy Spirit is the perfect bond uniting Father and Son in this eternal act of loving self-gift. Here is the essence of Love, God's very self - a Lover who gives himself over to the Beloved, the Beloved who receives, and both who are in turn united by Love itself. Unlike us creatures who begin life as individuals crying out for personal relationship, God *is* personal relationship: the Father who allows himself to be emptied into the beloved Son, the Son who is fully received by the Spirit of Love who eternally unites Father and Son in a timeless act of self-gift.

Made in this divine image

This mutual giving of selves is so abundant that God saw fit not to keep it to himself. In the Trinity's infinite wisdom, the Father, the Son and the Holy Spirit decided to share their love with an order of being infinitely distinct from themselves. Out of nothing, then, the Trinity lifted creatures so as to grant them a share in God. Each creature in its own way was brought about so as to praise the divine, all things were ordered to the communion of Creator and creation. All things are in some sense deiform, in that their existence and beauty confess a Creator who made them and guides them (cf. *Rom* 1:20). But not all things are equally alive, equally beautiful. As the story of creation unfolds, we see how the human person enjoys a special pre-eminence. All of creation is ordered to the communion of God with those creatures who are uniquely like him, with those creatures who alone are persons made in his image. Maximus the Confessor (d. 662) affirms such communion when he rightly saw how, "God created all beings with one end in mind: the union in Christ of humanity and divinity" (*Questions to Thalassius* §50). From the beginning of time, Christ's perfect union of divinity and humanity has been the goal toward which all created humans hasten, and such union demanded a unique creature capable of receiving God in a special and friendly way, God's own icons who have no more important vocation than to enter into loving union with him.

Genesis 1:26 provides us with the biblical basis of this truth: only the human person is made in God's image and likeness. Emblazoned with this divine stamp, we have been created in order to reflect the Triune God, and like any reflection, we are most real when we become like the model upon which we have been patterned. Herein lies the ultimate drama of human living. Unlike all the animals and angels, we stand as singularly made, as bridge creatures somewhat similar to the animals in that we live in time and space, but also like God in that we know and love, often transcending our bodily conditions to act freely and sacrificially. Having been made in God's image, no other relationship - no career, no family, no earthly success - can ever fully capture us. Is this not the source of much of our malaise? We have been brought out of nothing for the sake of divine communion and we easily allow ourselves to be fooled into thinking that we will find completion in a mortal or material comfort. Gregory of Nazianzus (d. 389/90) realized this struggle well: "The Word of God took a lump of newly created earth, formed it with his immortal hands into our shape and imparted life to it; for the spirit that he breathed into it is a flash of the invisible godhead. Thus from clay and breath was created humanity, the image of the Immortal... That is why in my earthly nature I am attached to life here below, while I also have in me a portion of the godhead; therefore is my heart tormented by the desire for the world to come" (*Dogmatic Poems* §8). An image remains frustrated as long as it fails to achieve union with its exemplar.

Becoming self-gift

This is how deification is the opposite of dehumanisation. In feeble attempts to unite ourselves with anything other than God, we act not like free persons but like those lesser creatures which surround us. "What made you establish the human person in so great a dignity? Certainly the incalculable love by which you have looked on your creature in yourself. You are taken with love for her; for by love indeed you created her, by love you have given her a being capable of tasting your eternal good" (St Catherine of Sienna, d. 1380, *Dialogue* 4.13; quoted at *CCC* 356). One of the fundamental insights of the Second Vatican Council (1963-65) formed the underlying message of John Paul II the Great's entire pontificate (1978-2005), that the human person "is the only creature on earth whom God willed for its own sake and thus can attain its full identity only in sincere self-giving" (*Gaudium et Spes* §24). As mentioned, God created man and woman for no other reason than his very own self. Grass he created for cows and cows for human hunger, but the human person is directed toward no other creature. Having been formed in God's Triune image, the rest of creation could never satisfy us, never fulfil us. Made to be like God, we find fulfilment only when we are transformed into perfect union with God, only when we live like the persons of the Trinity and give ourselves away in the self-gift of love.

Choosing selfish comfort over selfless charity, Adam and Eve lost the initial closeness God willed for them. Fooled to think that they could somehow "become gods" (*Gen* 3:5) without God, they forfeited the divine life offered to humanity. From afar God showed us how no law, no prophet, no human king, could ever capture our restless hearts and so he deigned to become a part of his own creation. A New Eve prepared the way for the New Adam and the second person of the Blessed Trinity was united to the fullness of humanity through the immaculate "yes" of the Blessed Virgin Mary. God became flesh (*John* 1:14) and took on all we humans are and experience (*Phil* 2:7-8). And now the type of communion Adam and Eve could have continued to enjoy with the Creator is far surpassed by the new way God can embrace us in Christ Jesus.

The Great Exchange

Humanity's divinisation is the result of Divinity's humanisation. The Church Fathers were unanimous on this exchange of God's humanity for our divinity: "Christ wanted to be what we are so that we could become what Christ is" (Cyprian, d. 258, *On the Vanity of Idols*, §11), "He clothed himself with our coarse mortality, that I might become God just as much as he became a man" (Gregory of Nazianzus, *Oration* 40.45), or in the words of Pope Leo the Great (d. 461), "The Redeemer became the Son of Man so that men and women could become sons and daughters of God" (*Sermon* 26). Our godliness is only possible because he who is eternally God became perfectly human, lived so as to defeat death, and now raises up a new creation through his sacred humanity. In fact, we can only fully appreciate the descent of God when we have come to understand the corresponding truth of our ascent as well. Through Mary's *fiat* - her 'yes' to God - and in Mary's womb, Jesus Christ became the perfect human. The only begotten Son of God attached our human nature to his divine personhood, and in so doing, deified all of humanity. As the Second Vatican Council teaches, the perfect humanity assumed by the Son of God "has been raised up to a divine dignity in our respect too...uniting himself in some fashion with every man and woman. He worked with human hands, He thought with a human mind, acted by human choice and loved with a human heart. Born of the Virgin Mary, He has truly been made one of us, like us in all things except sin" (*Gaudium et Spes* §22). The Son of God chose to be born of a perfect human mother so as to bring all of humanity into himself. He became human so we could become God!

As startling as all this may sound, it is really the core of Catholicism. At CCC 460 the words of some of the greatest thinkers of the Faith have been assembled to teach that:

> "The Word became flesh to make us 'partakers of the divine nature' (2 *Pet* 1:4). 'For this is why the Word became man, and the Son of God became the Son of man: so that man, by entering into communion with the Word and thus receiving divine sonship, might become a son of God' (St Irenaeus, d.c 200). 'For the Son of God became man so that we might become God' (St Athansius, d. 373). 'The only-begotten Son of God, wanting to make us sharers in his divinity, assumed our nature, so that he, made man, might make us gods" (St Thomas Aquinas, d. 1274)."

Christianity is singular in emphasizing this 'great exchange' - that out of unbounded generosity, God became like us so that, out of our innate desire for eternal life, we could become God. But in order to grasp accurately what the Church means here, we must first ask what she means when she calls God's faithful 'gods' themselves?

Sirach calls the patriarchs of Israel "godly men" (*Sirach* 44:1): at Psalm 8:6 we read that the human person is "a little less than a god", while Psalm 82:6 calls us "gods, sons and daughters of the Most High" - words Jesus consecrates by quoting them at Jn 10:34. However, we also read sacred scripture's threats against those who attempt to set themselves up as gods (*Gn* 3:5, *Is* 14). So, exactly how do we reconcile the non-negotiable monotheism of Christianity while its own Scripture and tradition unabashedly teach that the elect become God as well?

Becoming gods?

The difference between these two types of divinity, 'gods' and God, must be understood in terms of source and origin. A fire is hot due to its very own flames, whereas iron which is put in that fire becomes hot not because it is metal but because of the flames in which the iron participates. Christianity can call Christ's faithful 'gods' not because creatures somehow turn into

21

objects of worship, but by means of the perfect godliness made available in the human enfleshment of Jesus Christ: we can become like him and thereby reflect the eternal attributes otherwise reserved for God alone. In Christ, what was once reserved only for God, becomes calibrated to and thus wed to the creature. This is the greatest of all marriages, the divine to the human:

> "And so the bridegroom is one with the Father and one with the bride. Whatever he found in his bride alien to her own nature he took from her and nailed to his cross when he bore her sins and destroyed them on the tree. He received from her and clothed himself in what was hers by nature and gave her what belonged to him as God. He destroyed what was diabolical, took to himself what was human, and conferred on her what was divine" (Isaac of Stella, d. 1178, *Sermon* 11).

Whenever we love with true charity or forgive as the Father has forgiven us, we partake of his divinity which is never really 'ours' by nature but which has been made accessible to us in Jesus Christ's becoming one of us. The Son *is* God by nature and by right, God is precisely who he is; we 'become God' always and only through grace, through God's generous invitation to be refined and transformed in his divine life.

The essential difference between Christ's divinity and ours is that his is identifiable and connatural with who he is, God by his very being. The divinity to which we are called, however, is always extrinsic to our humanity and thus never 'ours', but is eternally experienced as a gift and as a state of being we could never merit or muster without the grace of God continually elevating and transforming our natural condition. So, although Christian deification has no problem in calling human persons 'gods', it does so while always walking between two extremes.

The first common error is to think that this is just pious, poetic talk, an honorific title void of any real significance. A common heresy of the Reformation was to reduce salvation to nothing more than Christ's covering up the sin which had taken root in oneself. In this view, the elect are externally justified but not internally sanctified - made righteous by God's decree, but never transformed into saints. The second misconception is to think that 'becoming gods' means ceasing to be a creature. We are all solitary beggars before the only One who has life in and of himself, and we will forever be contingent beings reliant upon divine grace for *everything*. The divinity for which we clamour is never 'ours' by right. It can never be experienced apart from the only One whose it is to grant. Unlike the Mormon doctrine of 'eternal progression' where one achieves his or her own 'Godship', or unlike

New Age creeds where one only has to realize the 'spark of divinity' within oneself, Christian godliness never renders us autonomous deities feigning independence, apart from the only true God. There is only one God, not a nameless number of Gods, nor is the infinite otherness between God and creature ever absolved.

The truth of deification stands in the middle of these two errors. By allowing us to enjoy his own life, God does not negate our finitude but, having made it his own in Christ Jesus, now elevates and transforms our creatureliness into something whole and perfect. In his freely-chosen poverty lies our freely-given richness. Accordingly, the Christian tradition could never refer to someone as a 'god' or 'divine' without simultaneously acknowledging his or her life in Jesus Christ. Christian deification says more about God's unmatched goodness in sharing his life than it does about the significance of the human person. The deification taught by the ancient Church points us to nothing other than the divine intimacy available in Christ's sacred humanity, to the only one in whom we are invited to place all of our desires and experiences.

Mary offers God all of us

At the Annunciation two marvellous events took place. First, when Mary spoke her total 'yes' to God, divinity was united with humanity. At this moment, the Second Person of the Trinity took the fullness of humanity to himself. How so? Because Mary was sinless, she was able to represent the whole of humanity. The first Eve, on the other hand, forfeited such universal motherhood when she turned away from divine communion. Consequently, humanity fell and was fractured, experienced as alienation from ourselves, others and God. In the divine plan, however, this fragmented and fallen humanity was restored in a New Eve, a new Mother containing all of humanity in herself. Thomas Aquinas argued that the angel of God sought the consent of the perfect human creature, "in order to show that there is a certain spiritual wedlock between the Son of God and human nature. Wherefore in the Annunciation the Virgin's consent was sought in the place of the consent of the entire human nature" (*Summa Theologiae* III.30.1). In Mary's sinlessness, the ocean of humanity had been again gathered, and in uniting himself to this new fountain of life, God thus made himself one with the whole sea of humanity and not merely with a single tributary.

The second event is a continuation of the first. Not only does Christ now unite his eternal divinity with his newly-acquired humanity in Mary, he makes his own divinity available to all of human persons. By uniting himself to the New Eve, God attaches himself to all of his children, and the Son now deifies all humanity. Having taken on the humanity in which we all participate, the Christ is now able to communicate his divinity to every human person. It is therefore accurate to say that although the Incarnation within Mary's womb of course remains unmatched and unrepeatable, its dynamics continue in the life of each Christian. The Son of God descended into the Virgin Mother in order to be joined to the whole of humanity and thereby make us who he is. By no means was this act of grace a 'one-off.' Christ continues to be born alive in billions and billions of souls, each with its unique history and desires. As the Incarnation is reproduced in the mystical Body of Christ, Christ's sacred humanity is thus extended and continued through his faithful members.

We are Christ's body on earth

The Son of God longs to identify himself with his Mystical Body on earth: "Saul, Saul," he cried from heaven, "why do you persecute *me*?" (*Acts* 9:4). Such identity is what allows us to be able to feed and to comfort the alienated Christ (cf. *Mt* 25:31-46); it is how St Paul knew it was Christ who does all things in him (cf. *Phil* 4:13), and how he can rejoice in his sufferings for the sake of Christ, and thereby in his own flesh, "fill up what is lacking in the afflictions of Christ on behalf of his body, which is the Church" (*Col* 1:24). One of the great bishops in late antiquity, Paulinus of Nola (d. 431), expresses this beautifully. Encountering Christ on every page of sacred scripture, Paulinus also saw how "Christ was slain by his brothers in Abel, mocked by his own son in Noah, exiled from his fatherland in Abraham, made a victim in Isaac, and made a slave in Jacob. He was sold in Joseph and exposed as an infant in Moses." It is always Christ, St Paulinus writes, who just as much as in the past as in the present day, "bears our afflictions and carries our grief; always is he, the Man covered with wounds for us, bearing that infirmity which we could never bear, even if we knew how to. For at this very moment, for us and in us, he endures the malice of the world, that endurance may have the victory and power be made perfect in infirmity. He, in you, suffers contempt, and it is he in you who is hated by the world" (*Letter* 38.3).

Think of it this way. As a Jewish male in early antiquity, Jesus could never have directly experienced, say, what it means to live in a post 9-11 world, or the demands of becoming a brand new (sleepless!) mother, or what it feels like to be a student trying to balance work, school and all the modern temptations inflicted upon us today. But the Lord of all history longs to dwell in every human soul, in each human life, enveloped by our free co-operation. He desires to descend from heaven to make humanity his dwelling so as to claim it again as his own, offering it back to his Father. This remains the Good News. Despite the modern-day threats of global terrorism, unjust regimes, homelessness and hunger, not to mention the chronic illnesses, deaths, divorces and disappointments of our own families, this is still the world where Love himself longs to incarnate himself.

An amazing homily delivered on Holy Saturday in the middle of the second century depicts this beautifully. From the beginning of Christian preaching, we hear that Christ descends into the depths of the human condition so as to unite all that is human with his divinity. The anonymous priest or bishop has us imagine Christ's descent into hell and there finds the first Adam asleep. There and then the Crucified One cries out to Adam, and to each of us today:

> "Awake, O sleeper, and rise from the dead, and I will give you light. I am your God, who for your sake have become your son. Out of love for you and for your descendants I now by my own authority command all who are held in bondage to come forth, all who are in darkness to be

enlightened, all who are sleeping to arise. I order you, O sleeper, to awake. I did not create you to be a prisoner in hell. Rise from the dead, for I am the life of the dead. Rise up, work of my hands, you who were created in my image. Rise, let us leave this place, for you are in me and I am in you; together we form only one person and we cannot be separated" (*Liturgy of the Hours*, Office of Readings for Holy Saturday [1976] 497).

Let us all arise! We have been made for neither hell nor earth, but for heaven. Let us all arise and begin to live there now. In our thoughts and in our actions, let us live as the pilgrims we are: men and women made for eternal beatitude in Christ. Let us live as Christ! Let us embrace his Church and all with which he feeds us there. Cast aside the fears and the struggles that keep us from embracing the fullness of the Faith. For Christ longs to identify his life with yours, to make you and him into one Christ praising the Father in the Spirit forever.

At a Christian's baptism the Son begins to praise the Father anew in each individual life, and as we mature we can freely collaborate with his unifying grace so as to make him incarnate in each of our daily lives. Now through your 'yes' and in your daily existence, Christ himself can live out the life of a nurse, a schoolteacher, a spouse. In all stages of his life, Christ continues to identify himself with his Mystical Body. In himself, of course, Christ is seated at the right hand of the Father in glory and suffers no more. However, in his Mystical Body on earth, in us, he lives a new life, he continues both to be persecuted as well as to triumph. Against much of the dry rationalism which aimed to reduce religion to a mere set of propositions, the seventeenth century 'French School of Spirituality' aimed to rejuvenate this living identity between Christ and his followers. Here the theologian and the mystic were one. One of the better known representatives of this way of thinking, John Eudes (d. 1680), helped others to see how each one of us is called to live the Divine Life:

> "We must strive to follow and fulfil in ourselves the various stages of Christ's plan as well as his mysteries and frequently beg him to bring them to completion in us and in the whole Church. For the mysteries of Jesus are not yet completely perfected and fulfiled. They are complete, in deed, in the person of Jesus, but not in us, who are his members, nor in the Church, which is his Mystical Body. The Son of God wills to give us a share in his mysteries and somehow to extend them to us. He wills to continue them in us and in his universal Church" (*On the Kingdom of Jesus* §3).

The Lord desires to reproduce his life in the lives of men and women, and to be transfigured as a teacher, a plumber, a doctor, or a cleaner. In this way he transfigures us by giving us a share in his grace and power.

What could be sweeter than knowing how Christ's love is so personal and so great that he is not satisfied with any distance between us but yearns to enter our very selves and make our lives his own? Could anything be dearer to us than the power with which he accomplishes such an exchange, making his life ours and our lives his? This is what, the greatest of all English converts, John Henry Cardinal Newman (d. 1890) called "the duty and the privilege of all disciples of our glorified Saviour, to be exalted and transfigured with Him; to live in heaven in their thoughts, motives, aims, desires, likings, prayers, praises, intercessions, even while they are in the flesh; to look like other men, to be busy like other men, to be passed over in the crowd of men, or even to be scorned or oppressed, as other men may be, but the while to have a secret channel of communication with the Most High, a gift the world knows not of; to have their life *hid* with Christ in God" (*Parochial & Plain Sermons*, vol. 6, no. 15). Through *sanctifying grace* God unites us with himself and makes his life our own. By giving us himself, a human soul is elevated into the divine life, and thus "gratuitously raised beyond all it deserves" (*CCC* 367). But precisely how does Christ change us into such new creatures?

Living Christ's life means being recreated in both body and soul. As God once blew a natural spirit into Adam (*Gen* 2:7), the New Adam breathes supernatural life, his own Spirit, into us (*Jn* 20:22). Christ makes his own life ours when he imparts his Holy Spirit into our souls, freeing us to form and extend his own divine life. The enfleshed God has come to send us his Spirit. Christ penetrates us and unites us to his own sacred humanity by means of the Holy Gift, the bond of Love, the Holy Spirit. The Spirit restores us in Christ, frees us from enslavement to sin, and imparts an everlasting joy as he unites us to the Father by making us like the Son.

New Creatures in the Spirit of Holiness

If we are going to become 'other Christs' we must possess the same Spirit as Christ. Becoming a child of God can be done only in God's Spirit. As we saw above, the workings of the Holy Trinity in this world imitate what God does eternally in himself. Within the Trinity, the Holy Spirit joins the Father and the Son in their perfect union of Love. Since it is the eternal role of the Spirit to unite persons, it fittingly belongs to his mission in history to continue unifying persons - now, however, human with divine persons. He is the agent of our union with God because the Holy Spirit is how God gives himself: eternally, as the Father gives himself to the Son and the Son empties himself into the Father, and in time, when that same Spirit of union dwells in us and unites us to the Father in the Son. For this is why the Holy Spirit has been sent: to penetrate a human life and unite it with the divine nature.

Reflecting on this mission of the Spirit in unifying humanity with God, John Paul II saw beautifully how the Holy Spirit first purifies our sinfulness, grants us a new life in Christ and thus makes us holy:

> "The Holy Spirit is 'Person-Love; he is Person-Gift'. This love given by the Father, received and reciprocated by the Son, is communicated to the one redeemed, who thus becomes a 'new man' (*Eph* 4:24), a 'new creation' (*Gal* 6:15). We Christians are not only purified from sin, but are also reborn and sanctified. We receive a new life, since we have become 'partakers of the divine nature' (2 *Pet* 1:4); we are 'called children of God; and so we are!' (*1 Jn* 3:1). It is the life of grace: the free gift by which God makes us partakers of this Trinitarian life" (*General Audience*, 22 July, 1998, §2).

Three distinct moments thus mark the movement of the Spirit in our lives. The first is to cleanse us from sin. We are purified so as to prepare us to receive the divine life more fully. Accordingly, the second moment is our divine adoption. Through God's unbounded graciousness, we imitate Christ in becoming a child of God the Father. From this follows the third moment: being made holy as we are lifted into the Trinitarian life itself. Let us now examine each of these three moments more fully.

The Scriptures teach that when the Holy Spirit comes, he will first "convict us of sin" (*John* 16:8). It is important to understand from the start that Christian conviction is the opposite of accusation or damnation. The Holy Spirit convicts us of sin in order to show us those crumbling parts of our hearts where God is not yet finished with us: "this same Spirit who brings sin to light is also the Consoler who gives the human heart grace for repentance and conversion" (*CCC* 1433). It is the Spirit of transparency who urges us to meet the Father of Mercies in the Sacrament of Penance and Reconciliation. This is why the Spirit of God 'convicts' us. He unveils our sins for no other reason than to prompt us to return to the Father of all mercy with unfaded trust in his perfect and unshakeable love. To convict here does not mean to denounce or disparage. The Spirit convicts us of the truth, of the whole truth: that of God's unconditional care as well as the truth of our own aversion to such divine tenderness. Satan, on the other hand, is the one who condemns (cf. *Rom* 8:1, *Rev* 12:9). The enemy of our human nature points out our sins only to exploit our deepest fears that maybe, after all, we really are no good, that we really are not loveable in our brokenness. Satan accuses us and persuades us to think that if we are really ever going to be accepted, we must "become like gods" (*Gen* 3:5) and do away with our vulnerability and weakness. What lies!

Have you ever noticed for whom Christ reserves his strongest words? He never speaks sharply to sinners, he never glares at tax collectors or prostitutes. He is never harsh to the weak and struggling. Rather, he saves his fiercest words for the hypocrites - the professional religious - who think and act as if they are not in need of a Saviour. Hypocrisy comes from a Greek term meaning 'to speak out from underneath' and was originally a word used to describe what happens from behind an actor's mask. The hypocrites speak out from under their self-righteousness. They deny Christ's Messiahship because they refuse to see that they too stand in need of saving. The poor and the wretched, the weak and empty-handed, though, rush to Christ and fervently embrace his message because they realize that here is the one who has finally come in the flesh to save them. Are not our hearts the same? Those places where we feel confident and self-assured are usually the last places we ask Jesus to save, but those tombs and prisons hidden deeply away prove to be precisely where he is able to work his greatest wonders.

If this is the case, why do we feel so unlovable so often? We must recognize that at the heart of living the Christ-life is the recognition that he has first loved us, not that we have loved him. "In this is love: not that we have loved God, but that he loved us and sent his Son as expiation for our sins. Beloved, if God so loved us, we also must love one another" (*1 Jn* 4:10-11). The Spirit reorients our eyes, taking them off our brokenness and pointing them toward God's unmatched love and care. "When we think of ourselves we are perturbed and filled with a salutary sadness. And when we think of the Lord, we are revived to find consolation in the joy of the Holy Spirit. From the first we derive fear and humility, from the second hope and love" (Bernard of Clairvaux, d. 1153, *Sermon 5 on Diverse Topics*, §5). The Holy Spirit teaches us that the Father's care is precisely what indeed makes us loveable. We are loved because God is Love and it is his nature which renders us pleasing. This is the stuff of the oldest of tales: it is the love of the princess which brings out the humanity of the frog, the tenderness of the woman which creates the man selfishly surrounded by the beast. The Holy Spirit does the same with us: it is his love which transforms us. It is he who makes us lovable. We are first accepted by God because of his nature, not ours.

Becoming a child of God

In this way the Holy Spirit leads us to see who God is more clearly. He has come to open up our hearts wide enough so as to know God as Father, as *Abba* (*Rom* 8:15). The Father's divine plan for us is to extend his paternity: not to beget us out of his own being, of course, but to make us his sons and daughters out of grace. In the Spirit we come to know the divine more in terms of personal relationship. God is no longer some nondescript power somewhere 'out there'. In our new life, God becomes our Father, the Son becomes our brother - our friend, our other self - and we soon realize how the Holy Spirit is our helper, our consoler, the love and the prayers moving deeply within us. This is how we are to pray: *to* the Father, *with* the Son and *in* the Spirit. But could we now say: to the Father, *as* a child of God, in the Spirit? As we become Christ, we pray as he does, we stay awake with him, praying with the same confidence and "filial boldness" (*CCC* 2610) as the Son himself.

This new life illumines us to see God as he most truly exists: Father, Son and Spirit. Whereas all creation participates in God, in whom we all "live, move, and have our being" (*Acts* 17:28), the just soul is made a child of the Most High and is therefore enabled *to love the Father as the Son in the Spirit*.

In making us like his Son, the Spirit extends the Father's paternity, and we who are "gazing with unveiled face on the glory of the Lord, are being transformed into the same image from glory to glory, as from the Lord who is the Spirit" (*2 Cor* 3:18). Although the genetic makeup is different - Christ being Son by nature and we children by grace - we are no less son or daughter. Furthermore, God has seen to it that we need not belong to a 'single parent' family. In this adoption process he has provided the best of all possible mothers, his own! As she begot the Son of God in her flesh through the work of the Holy Spirit, she regenerates new sons and daughters through her Son's flesh, again through the same unifying, deifying work of God's Spirit. On earth Mary is 'Mother Church', the one whom God entered in order to become a man and the same Mother whom we all enter each day so as also to be made into children of God.

But what does it mean when we say that the Spirit *makes* us sons and daughters of God? Every Sunday we recite the Creed which was written by the Bishops at the Council of Nicaea (325 AD) and then expanded at the Council of Constantinople (381 AD), professing that we believe in "one Lord, Jesus Christ, the only Son of God, eternally begotten of the Father, God from God, Light from Light, true God from true God, *begotten not made*, of one Being with the Father." Christ is the "only" Son of God because he is the only one "begotten" by the Father: out of the same substance, equal in power and might, coming from but not somehow after the Father in a timeless begetting. This is the primary difference between begetting and making something. To beget something means that the begetter and the begotten are equal in nature. God begets God, mice beget mice, human parents beget human children, and so on. What happens to us in the Holy Spirit is that we are *made not begotten* children of God. To make something is to give some pre-existing object a new nature: wood is made into a table, cloth is made into a shirt. The maker is always and everywhere prior in time and superior in being to that which has been made. We are made sons and daughters of God as the Holy Spirit graciously brings us into the familial life of the Trinity. We remain creatures but creatures who have now been recreated to live anew by participating in the life of the divine. Our Catechism attributes this newness of life in a special way to the Holy Spirit labouring inside each of us:

> "Through the power of the Holy Spirit we take part in Christ's Passion by dying to sin, and in his Resurrection by being born to a new life; we are members of his Body which is the Church, branches grafted onto the vine which is himself: 'God gave himself to us through his Spirit. By the participation of the Spirit, we become communicants in the divine nature...' For this reason, those in whom the Spirit dwells are divinised" (*CCC* 1988).

Being grafted onto the Lord points us to the connection between Christ and his disciples - so close that we form a single organism, so diverse that we grow in perfection as we all grow in our various vocations. It is the Holy Spirit that blends us into Christ's life, a process known as a particularly Catholic concept: sanctification.

The life of sanctification

To be 'sanctified' comes from the Latin, 'to be made holy', and forms the core of our teaching on the Christ life: we are made into holy temples of God's Spirit. Because of his love for us, God does not will that we go on struggling and stumbling in our sinfulness and confusion. So he not only releases us from evil, he continues to make us more and more like himself. He loves us enough to change us!

Sanctification is our deification, our holiness. One of the greatest 20th century spiritual masters, Columba Marmion (d. 1923), an Irish Benedictine monk who lived most of his life in the Maredsous Abbey in Belgium, came to understand how holiness was "the conformity of all our being to God; it is the *amen* said by the whole being and its faculties to all the rights of God; it is the *fiat* ('may it be done') full of love, whereby the whole creature responds, unceasingly and unfalteringly, to all the Divine Will" (*Christ the Ideal of the Monk* [1922] 375). Sanctification means becoming wholly transparent before the Father, allowing him to see and to have all of us: every thought, every desire, action, word and dream. Many falter or fail to live the Christ-life deeply because they have been negligent in fostering an active devotion and closeness to the Holy Spirit. He is the invisible nearness of God, union personified, the permeating presence of the divine who can inform all of our thoughts and guide each of our decisions. Once we have allowed our entire life to become such a prayer, such a *fiat*, then can the Father begin to reproduce his Son's life and features within us. Holiness is realisable only when we enter into this Great Exchange: allowing God to possess our life fully so he can give us his life in return. We must die to all that is not his within us and allow ourselves to become '*filii in Filio*', daughters and sons in the Son. As we grow into God's family we come to understand how the Holy Spirit is the permanent seal on our certificates of adoption, signed by the Father in the life-giving blood of his only Son!

Seeking the Grace of Union

So where do we go from here? How do we begin to seek the renewal of our hearts and the union God wills for us? Let us begin by acknowledging that this is all grace. Nothing is ultimately ours. There can be no growth without God's willing and granting it. Beg the Father of tenderness to make you evermore his child and to send you the fullness of his Spirit. Let us conclude by examining five areas essential to growing in the Christ-life. You may find that one of these areas has been neglected or has fallen into coldness or confusion. Again, ask the Holy Spirit to guide you through each of these areas and show you what it is he wills.

Divine intimacy

First off, do not be afraid! Where do you secretly fear God's closeness? This is a point worth pondering. To some degree, we all fear the intimacy of another. At some level, we know that allowing another into our lives means that we can no longer remain in control. C.S. Lewis (d. 1963) writes very beautifully:

"To love at all is to be vulnerable. Love anything and your heart will certainly be wrung and possibly be broken. If you want to make sure of keeping it intact, you must give your heart to no one, not even to an animal...lock it up safe in the casket or coffin of your selfishness. But in that casket - safe, dark, motionless, airless - it will change. It will not be broken; it will become unbreakable, impenetrable, irredeemable" (*The Four Loves*, ch. 6).

Personal union always demands that we make space in our heart for another, for another set of ideas, plans and pains. As such, charity demands courage. Loving means admitting that the things we hold sacred are in the end only dross, and it will certainly mean living for one who is wholly other, one whom we cannot, must not, control. We cannot enter heaven by halves, and the Spirit of God has been sent to claim all of us; not only our 'good stuff', only those cleaner parts of our hearts we think God is interested in but all of us, our fears, our darkness, our weakness, even our sin. Disappointment is not a divine attribute. God could not let you down even if he somehow wanted to. Trust in him. Do not be afraid.

Becoming God's Love

Secondly, learn Christian charity. If we are going to imitate and thereby become Christ, we must strive to love as he loves. This is the most essential factor in our total union. True charity is not an abstract, ethereal feeling reserved for a distant object. Rather, it is a commitment to gaze tenderly on all we meet and to speak and work for their eternal good. It is to realise how Christ has hidden himself in each of us. In her classic work on the Mother of God, the English writer and mystic, Caryll Houselander (d. 1954), observes how:

> "There could not be a more ingenious way than the one he has devised, his way of hiding himself in us, revealing his presence in our necessities, so that we can only find him by obeying his commandment, 'Little children, love one another!' He hides and can be found, not only in a child, but in your child; not only in a friend, but in your friend; not only in a servant, but in your servant: could there be easier access to him than your child, your friend, your servant?" (*Reed of God*, 'Our Seeking', 106).

Look around, see those in whom your heart rejoices and see how God has chosen to love you. Quit spiritualising the embodied Christ. See his living presence. Do not feel guilty for loving thus but do learn to consecrate this love. Let it never become earthly but know that love, to be worthy of eternity, must be informed by and directed toward heavenly love. If we love with the love of God, we love forever. If we try to love from our own emotional egoism, someday we shall hold that person no more. Have you ever prayed while flipping through a cherished photo album? Try it. Do not worry that it is not 'religious' or 'spiritual' enough. Let these faces become the divine mirror in which you see your worth. Those around you are the means through whom God has chosen to love you and the way he invites you to love him.

Entering the silence

This is the third area you must constantly re-evaluate in your life. How are you praying? There is no substitute for daily, silent contemplative prayer. Begin with 10 minutes each morning. Pick a peaceful place, decide whether you should kneel, sit or stand, and then set your watch for 10 minutes so as to avoid looking up and checking how long you still have to go. Carefully read the Gospel for that day and then allow it to play out in your imagination: what is the scene, do you identify with any of the characters, what is Jesus saying to you, how do these words make you feel and why, what would you change about the story?

Rely on your life experiences as the events God is using to draw you into greater communion with him. Relish the everyday and see how the mundane is charged with God's presence. Seek silence, but if all you can muster is driving to work one day without any radio or music, do that. When we pray it is important to recognise that we cannot always control what comes in and out of our heads, but we can control our bodies. If we have told God we give him the next 20 minutes in Church, this one commute without distraction, this one walk around the block in meditation, stick to it regardless of how 'long' the time may seem or regardless of how heavy-going it may become.

If we continue on a life of regular prayer, we will soon find that time goes by much quicker and, much more to the point, that our love longs to be perfect, our emotions faultless and our thoughts radiant with joy. We will be torn from our limitations of selfishness and petty jealousies, gone will be those nagging fears and insecurities. We should begin to notice how we have, over time, become more focused, more integrated and less anxious, less tugged by nagging, sinful habits. We will be human as Christ became human: perfect in reaching out to the other and thus able to receive the fullness of that other. We will no longer be half-hearted creatures running around trying to fill ourselves with diversions and less than wholly satisfying flirtations. We will be so giving of self that we will experience only the fullness of self. The more we grow in the Spirit of love, the more we become aware of one another. The more we live the deified life, as both means and end of our existence, the more sympathetic we become to those who struggle around us, to all those men and women who long for the intimacy and the security life in Christ brings. Attuned to the Spirit through years of monastic silence, Thomas Merton (d. 1968), an American Trappist, on a day trip to the local big city, found himself experiencing this unity between God's people.

> "In Louisville, at the corner of Fourth and Walnut, in the centre of the shopping district, I was suddenly overwhelmed with the realization that I loved all those people, that they were mine and I theirs, that we could not be alien to one another even though we were total strangers...My solitude...is not my own, for I see now how much it belongs to them - and that I have a responsibility for it in their regard, not just in my own. It is because I am one with them that I owe it to them to be alone, and when I am alone they are not 'they' but my own self. There are no strangers!" (*Conjectures of a Guilty Bystander* [1989] 156-58).

This is why the Faith is never 'mine' or 'yours' - it is a gift from God and must be received humbly, handled truthfully. Dissent has no place in the Christ life: we are one body gathered under one Head, and the actions of each affects all of its members.

The people of God

Our relationship to the Church is the fourth area we must examine. How do I understand and enter into the sacramental life of the Church? How do I regard her moral teachings, especially the wholly counter-cultural truths such as the atrocity of abortion or the sinfulness of artificial birth control? As God's beloved spouse, the one, holy, catholic and apostolic Church has providentially emerged out of the rubble of all other ancient religions. She alone has found a place in the souls of men and women in every age and in every land. All parts of the globe have recognized the joy promised in her teachings and all have witnessed the sanctity lived out in the lives of her saints. Here is the perfect way meant for all.

The Church is why Jesus was predestined to become "the firstborn among many brothers and sisters" (*Rom* 8:29), why he became the firstborn of the great assembly (cf. *Heb* 12:23), that living structure which his own body forms into a sacred temple, a dwelling place of God (cf. *Eph* 2:21-22). This is why the Father has established him as "the head of the body, the Church" (*Col* 1:18), so as to hide his divine humanity in each of us. Being infinite in wisdom means possessing perfect foresight. Jesus Christ no doubt realized that he would have to build up a body like his own in order to continue and expand his divine presence on earth. Never content living in isolation from anyone, Jesus knew that, once ascended, his life-giving flesh must still be made available to those who were to come after him. This is why he founded (cf. *Mt* 16:18) and promised to guide a Church that was universal (in Greek, *katholikos*), so all people of all times could have a share in his Mystical Body.

He therefore instituted the Sacraments so those who were to come after him could enjoy equal access to his enfleshed Presence. All the sacraments aim toward a three-fold union: integrity within each person, communion with Christ's Body of saints and, above all, union with God. Such a life begins at our baptism. "These are therefore the effects of Baptism: to set free from sins, to reconcile man to God, to make man one with God, to open the eyes that souls might perceive the divine ray - in sum, to prepare for the life to come...it is the beginning of the life in Christ, and causes men to exist, live, and excel in true life and being" (Nicholas Cabasilas, d. after 1387, *The Life in Christ* II.22 [1974] 101). Baptism heals the division of sin within each soul as well as between individuals. From the moment we are baptized the Trinity takes up a new life within us and continues the Father's begetting of the Son in the Spirit in our very souls! The Spirit now empowers us to pray and love *Abba* in a way (cf. *Rom* 8:15) we could not have before we were immersed into the waters made holy by Christ's own descent into the Jordan. Every time you dip your hand into a holy water font and cross yourself in the name of the Holy Trinity, you too are plunged into the Jordan, renewing your baptismal covenant, and hopefully hearing that you are God's beloved in whom he is well pleased.

Baptism unites all Christians, regardless of denominational differences. We pray that we will again be able to share the same Eucharistic table, that we may again be one as the Father and Son are one (cf. *Jn* 17:11). The Spirit of divine adoption infused into our souls at baptism makes all Christians brothers and sisters: "For in one Spirit we were all baptized into one body, whether Jews or Greeks, slaves or free persons, and we were all given to drink of one Spirit" (*1 Cor* 12:13). If we who are in the flesh wish to grow more and more in the divine nature, there is no other way than by drawing close to the enfleshed God. Ask yourself this question: "How is the presence of the Holy Spirit different in my life to the presence of Jesus Christ, God made flesh?" Christ is God-made-flesh and his presence can no longer be explained by some vague spiritual ubiquity. This is the quandary that literally changed my life: if we today profess to be saved by the flesh of Christ, where is that flesh today? How do *I* walk to Calvary, how do *I* encounter the risen, incarnate Lord? The Church's Eucharist holds the answer. For without the Eucharist at the centre of all worship, Christianity would be a mean trick. We would otherwise be forced into merely remembering the biblical Christ or only able to anticipate the Christ yet to come: without his *real presence*, the enfleshed Son of God could not truly be encountered here and now.

St Athanasius translates his famous saying, "God became man so men could become gods" into a Eucharistic formula: "We are divinized, not by partaking of the body of any man, but by receiving the Body of the Word himself" (*Letter* 60.4). Christ continues his presence among us so as to enter us and make his life ours. No distance is too great for his longing heart:

> "For you I was covered with blows and spittle... but I have pursued you, I ran after you, in order to hold you, and I united myself to you and bound you to myself. 'Eat me', I said, 'and drink me.' Is it not enough that I possess your first fruits in the heavens? Does that not satisfy the desire? I also descended to earth, not only to mingle myself with you but to intertwine myself with you. I am eaten. I am broken into pieces, in order that the mingling, the blending, the union may be profound...I no longer want anything between the two of us. I desire that we two may be one" (John Chrysostom, d. 407, *Homily on 1 Tim* 15.4).

Likening the Host we receive in holy communion to that divine piece of coal given to the prophet Isaiah (cf.

Is 6) so as to purge his sin and open his mouth, John Damascene (d. 750) also exhorts us to "draw near" to the Blessed Sacrament, "with an ardent desire, and with our hands held in the form of a cross let us receive the Body of the Crucified One: and let us apply our eyes and lips and brows and partake of the divine coal, in order that the fire of the longing that is in us, with the additional heat derived from the coal may utterly consume our sins and illumine our hearts, and that we may be inflamed and deified by the participation in the divine fire" (*On the Orthodox Faith*, 4.13).

Is there Eucharistic Adoration near where you live or work? There is perhaps no greater way to pray than before the Blessed Sacrament. 1 Jn 3:2 promises us that we shall become like God because we shall know him as he is. When we know something, in a certain way, we become it. That is, beholding something with our senses creates a natural affinity between ourselves and that upon which we gaze. It happens whenever we are immersed in a novel or in a movie: we actually 'enter' that story and are conscious of such a change only when someone startles us. Spending time in front of the Eucharist is a lot like that: there, unlike anywhere else, we can be drawn into the life of the Lord and unite ourselves with his sacred Body. There we can begin to picture our lives as a gradual receptivity of properly divine attributes - a universal compassion, a fiery love, an unquenchable joy. A second century collection of aphorisms has us imagine the following:

> "See! The Lord is your Mirror.
> Open your eyes. Look into It.
> And learn what your face is like!"
> (*The Odes of Solomon* §13).

The Mirror is that Sacred Host staring back at us. He shows us both our human worth as well as other truths that we would rather ignore: here is the face we have spat upon, here is the one whom we have all denied. Fear not, little flock, it pleases the Father to give you his Son, to hand over to you his entire Kingdom (cf. *Lk* 12:32).

The sacraments continue the life of the Trinity in time: they cleanse us from sin, they form our loves with a new wisdom and bring us into contact with living divinity. Purification, illumination and union are the three traditional stages of the spiritual life, and if you have experienced any of the Church's sacraments, you likewise have participated in this new life. The day I was ordained a priest, I was changed but I did not cease to be human or to be myself. Nonetheless, a new life was given me, manifested by a new ability to perform sacred actions. Just that morning God could not have relied on me to absolve sins or to consecrate bread and wine into the Saviour's precious Body and Blood. Holy Orders gave me a new way of being externalised by an entirely new way of living out my day. Such a new life may be most obvious with Holy Orders but this happens with every Sacrament. Before you were baptized you could not properly believe the Gospel, hope in Christ or love as God loves. Immersed into the Triune life through Baptism, these virtues were infused into your soul and you literally became a 'new creature'. You were transformed into a Christian and your behaviour became 'super-human', in that Christian faith, hope and charity are really sacred actions which no mortal can alone perform. At my ordination, my hands became the hands with which Christ continued the Last Supper, the words I freely spoke in the confessional have become the words of absolution Christ himself speaks so as to forgive sins and heal hearts. At your baptism you became the human instrument with which God chose to continue to manifest his presence and power in the world; at your marriage, you became the enfleshed heart with which God would manifest his nuptial love for the world, and so on.

In his incarnation and brazen entry into the human condition, Jesus Christ has become like us, a new Adam who has come to give birth to a new race of men and women. The Son of God has come not just to improve our lot but to change it, not just to improve our vision but to give us completely new eyes! To quote C.S. Lewis again: "God became man to turn creatures into sons [and daughters]: not simply to produce better men of the old kind but to produce a new kind of man. It is not like teaching a horse to jump better and better but like turning a horse into a winged creature" (*Mere Christianity* [1958] 167). The Church is the arena where these changes are brought about, the place where we become one with Christ.

Like any Mother, this Church has a face: Mary. Draw close to the first deified human person. Mary provided Christ's perfect and sanctified human nature. Jesus, a divine person with a fully human nature, in turn gave Mary, a human person, a full participation in the divine life. She is who we all hope to become. "Mary, now in heaven, God's design for her completely fulfiled, is the flower and first fruit of the Church and of creation, which in her is already Christified, divinized." (Chiara Lubich, *An Introduction to the Abba School*, 28). Mary is the heart of created union. In her "full of grace" (cf. *Lk* 1:28) we see the destiny of the perfectly integrated human person, in her 'yes' (cf. *Lk* 1:38) she unites all of humanity with divinity, and in her "all generations shall call me blessed" (cf. *Lk* 1:48), every human person is brought under the same faith in worship of the one true God. Talk to Mary. Ask her who she is for you and who you can be for her.

Prayer for union with God

Heavenly Father,

thank you for this gift of life and the wonders of your world.

Thank you even more for the new life promised in your Son, the Lord Jesus Christ.

He is what I am to become.

So, Jesus, sweet and gentle Teacher, form your heart in mine,

And grant me a share in your divine life.

Burn away all my fear, coldness, and confusion.

Come to me in your Blessed Sacrament and send me your Holy Spirit, the only One who can teach me to pray as a true child of God.

May all your Holy Angels watch over me and cast out the accuser who tries to keep me tied to those old lies about myself and about you.

Mother Mary, show me who you are and what you mean for my life as a follower of your Son. You were the first to hold him deep inside, pray also for me, that I am given this grace of interiority, allowing me to see your Son in all I do and in all I meet.

Most Loving Trinity, grant me the desire to be totally yours,

through Christ the Lord.

Amen

Futher Reading

Keep reading and studying. For some helpful literature on deepening this sense of the Christ life within you, you may want to read these works or check out the following websites:

Jean Borella, *The Sense of the Supernatural* (Edinburgh: T&T Clark, 1998), a superb introduction into the question of 'nature' and 'grace' and their inseparability.

M. Eugene Boylan, *This Tremendous Lover*, currently reprinted by Christian Classics in Allen, Texas, now in its 34th printing, intent on restoring the image of Christ as a lover of souls, as the spouse of our entire lives.

Michael Casey, *Fully Human - Fully Divine: An Interactive Christology* (Liguori, Missouri, Liguori Publications, 2004), a guide through the Gospel of Mark but one that stresses how Mark's portrayal of Jesus is aimed at effecting the deified life in his readers; filled with unmatchable spiritual insights.

Olivier Clément, *The Roots of Christian Mysticism* (New York: New City Press, 1993), an anthology with Patristic references treating divine union and other sacred mysteries of the Christ life.

Abbot Columba Marmion, *Christ the Life of the Soul*. This book is out of print but can be found on various sites on the internet. It is an indispensable classic in exploring the deified life.

Panayiotis Nellas, *Deification in Christ: The Nature of the Human Person* (Crestwood, New York: St. Vladimir's Seminary Press, 1987), a nice combination of original thoughts by this theologian from Greece as well as a comprehensive anthology of Patristic sources.

Norman Russell, *The Doctrine of Deification in the Greek Patristic Tradition* (Oxford University Press, 2004), the new standard for scholars taking us through the various views of how humans live and describe the divine life.

John Saward, *Cradle of Redeeming Love: The Theology of the Christmas Mystery* (San Francisco, California: Ignatius Press, 2002), from Oxford's own Fr. Saward is a beautiful reflection on how Christmas shows us how God has become human so humans can become God.

Matthias Scheeben, *The Glories of Divine Grace*, reprinted by Tan Books and Publishers, Rockford, Illinois, an excellent work done by this 19th century priest on the effects of grace in our lives.

There are also various websites, that while perhaps not treating deification directly, contain some very valuable messages:

www.catholiceducation.org
www.catholic-pages.com
www.catholic.com
www.godspy.com
www.secondspring.co.uk
www.salvationhistory.com
www.theveil.net